CONTENTS

Preface .... **4.**

An introduction to the transformative power of sales and what readers can expect from the book.

Part I: The Foundations of Selling

1. **The Essence of Selling** .... **7.**
   a. Why Sales is the Lifeblood of Business
   b. The Role of Conviction and Product Knowledge
   c. Overcoming the Five Barriers to Sales
2. **Powerful Sales Strategies** .... **15.**
   a. Key Formulas and Techniques for Success
   b. Lead Scoring and Prioritization
   c. Using the SPANCO Framework
3. **Advanced Sales Techniques** .... **29.**
   a. Emotional Decision-Making and Psychology
   b. Trial Closes, Conditional Closes, and Other Advanced Techniques
   c. The Importance of Persistent Follow-Ups

Part II: Digital Sales and Tools

4. **Digital Strategies for Success** .... 40.
    a. Transitioning from Offline to Online Sales
    b. Building an Engaging Social Media Presence
    c. High-Converting Landing Pages
5. **Online Sales Tools** .... 52.
    a. Tracking Competitors and Analyzing Market Trends
    b. Managing Your Online Reputation
    c. Using CRM Systems and Automation Tools

Part III: Building Relationships and Long-Term Success

6. **Sales Closing Techniques** .... 64.
    a. Mastering the Art of the Close
    b. Handling Objections Gracefully
    c. Using AIDA to Close Effectively
7. **Building Customer Loyalty** .... 75.
    a. Creating Emotional Connections with Customers
    b. Designing Loyalty Programs and Encouraging Repeat Purchases
    c. Leveraging Feedback for Continuous Improvement
8. **Discounts and Schemes** .... 85.

    a. Strategic Use of Discounts to Drive Sales
    b. Avoiding the Discount Trap
    c. Measuring the Impact of Promotions

Part IV: Scaling and Future Growth

9. **Customer-Centric Sales .... 96.**
   a. Understanding and Solving Customer Needs
   b. Personalizing the Sales Experience
   c. The Golden Circle Framework
10. **Scaling Your Sales Operations .... 107.**
    a. Building a Scalable Sales Framework
    b. Expanding into New Markets
    c. Optimizing the Sales Funnel
11. **Conclusion and Future Directions .... 119.**
    a. Recapping Key Lessons
    b. Actionable Next Steps for Implementing Strategies
    c. The Path to Mastering the Art of Selling

Closing Note: A Message from the Author .... 126.

A heartfelt message reflecting on the journey of writing this book, thanking the readers, and inspiring them for future success.

PREFACE

In the ever-evolving world of business, sales is more than just a function—it's the pulse that drives success, growth, and transformation. Regardless of the size or nature of a business, selling effectively is what bridges the gap between potential and achievement. Yet, for many, sales remains an elusive art, clouded by misconceptions and uncertainty.

This book, **"The Art of Selling: Strategies to Transform Your Business,"** is your definitive guide to mastering this vital skill. It demystifies the process of selling, breaking it down into actionable strategies and timeless principles. Whether you're a seasoned professional looking to refine your techniques or a budding entrepreneur aiming to scale your business, this book provides a roadmap to achieving sales excellence.

Each chapter is designed to build your understanding and enhance your capabilities. We begin by establishing the foundation—exploring why sales is the lifeblood of every business and the key mindsets and skills required to succeed. From there, we delve into powerful strategies and advanced techniques, such as leveraging psychology, handling objections, and crafting value-driven sales approaches.

As the digital landscape transforms the way businesses operate, we guide you through strategies for success in the online world, from building an engaging social media presence to using cutting-edge tools and technologies to scale your sales operations. You'll learn how to close deals effectively, retain loyal customers, and design promotions that enhance value without eroding profitability.

Finally, this book equips you to think beyond transactions. It's about understanding your customers, solving their problems, and building lasting relationships. Sales is not just about closing deals—it's about creating connections that drive loyalty and growth.

"The Art of Selling: Strategies to Transform Your Business" is more than a guide; it's a tool for transformation. By the end of this book, you won't just sell—you'll inspire, solve, and succeed.

Welcome to the journey of mastering the art of selling. Let's transform your business together.

Chapter 1
The Essence of Selling

Sales is the lifeline of every business. Without it, even the most groundbreaking ideas or innovative products would wither away. Selling is more than a skill; it's an art—a delicate balance of understanding people, building trust, and delivering value. Yet, many misunderstand the true nature of selling. They see it as persuasion or pushing a product. In reality, selling is about solving problems and making life better for the customer.

This chapter lays the foundation for your sales journey. Whether you're an entrepreneur trying to scale your business or a professional aiming to close bigger deals, the principles here will guide you toward mastery.

Sales as a Driver of Transformation

Imagine you have a fantastic product or service. You've invested time, resources, and passion into it. But here's the harsh truth: none of it matters if you can't sell. Sales is the vehicle that turns potential into results. It's what connects your ideas to the people who need them most.

Here's something profound: sales is not just about transactions; it's about trust. Customers don't buy from companies—they buy from people they trust. They look for confidence, conviction, and clarity in their decision-making process.

Golden Statement:

"Sales is about transferring your enthusiasm and belief to your customer."

Building the Foundation: Product Knowledge + Conviction

At the heart of every successful sale lies this simple yet powerful formula:

Product Knowledge + Conviction = Sales

Let's break this down:

- **Product Knowledge**: You must know your product or service inside out. Understand its features, benefits, and how it solves specific problems for your customers. Knowledge isn't just power; it's credibility.
- **Conviction**: Believing in your product is just as important. Without conviction, your words lack the energy and passion to inspire confidence.

Consider this: would you buy something from someone who doesn't seem sure about what they're selling? Probably not. Conviction is the invisible thread that ties your product to your customer's trust.

Example:

Imagine you're selling an air purifier. If you know how it filters pollutants and can demonstrate its impact on indoor air quality, you can speak confidently. When you combine that knowledge with genuine belief in the product's ability to improve lives, your customer is far more likely to buy.

Golden Statement:

"Confidence is contagious. When you believe in your product, your customer will too."

The Five Barriers to Sales

Every salesperson faces objections, and it's essential to understand them. These are the five common reasons customers hesitate to buy:

1. **No Need**: They don't see how your product fits into their lives.
2. **No Hurry**: There's no urgency to make the purchase.
3. **No Desire**: The product doesn't excite or attract them.
4. **No Trust**: They don't trust you, your product, or your company.
5. **No Money**: They perceive the product as too expensive.

Overcoming these barriers requires empathy and strategy. For instance:

- To tackle "no need," highlight how your product solves a specific problem.
- For "no trust," share testimonials or offer guarantees that build credibility.

Golden Statement: *"Every 'no' is an opportunity to uncover the real objection and turn it into a 'yes.'"*

The Journey to Sales Mastery

Sales mastery doesn't happen overnight—it's a journey of learning, adapting, and consistently applying proven strategies. This journey unfolds in two stages:

1. **Stage 1: Laying the Foundation**

This stage is all about understanding the basics. Learn how to connect with customers, manage your leads, and track performance. Think of it as building the rocket that will propel your sales efforts.

2. **Stage 2: Advanced Implementation**

Here, you refine your craft with advanced techniques like consultative selling and persuasive closing. It's about achieving sustainable growth through consistency and follow-through.

Example:

A small business owner selling handmade candles starts by understanding their audience's preferences (Stage 1). As they grow, they implement loyalty programs and upselling techniques to retain and expand their customer base (Stage 2).

Golden Statement:

"The basics ignite your rocket; advanced techniques keep it soaring."

Bringing It All Together

Selling is an art that blends science, empathy, and conviction. The formula for success isn't complicated, but it demands focus and effort. When you combine product knowledge with belief, and when you commit to the journey of continuous improvement, the results are transformational.

Reflection for the Reader:

- Do you truly understand your product, and can you explain its benefits with confidence?
- How do you overcome objections like "no trust" or "no hurry"?
- Are you ready to embark on the two-stage journey of sales mastery?

Key Takeaways

1. Sales is about solving problems and transferring your belief to the customer.
2. Build trust by combining product knowledge with conviction.
3. Address objections thoughtfully to guide customers toward a decision.

Golden Statement: *"Selling is not about convincing—it's about connecting."*

Chapter 2
Powerful Sales Strategies

Introduction

Sales is not just about pushing products or services—it's about solving problems, creating value, and building trust. However, achieving this requires more than enthusiasm; it demands structured strategies. In this chapter, we delve into nine powerful sales strategies that form the backbone of successful selling. These strategies, when understood and applied correctly, can transform your approach to sales and help you connect with customers at a deeper level.

1. Conviction in Product Knowledge

The first and most important strategy is mastering product knowledge. To sell effectively, you need to know your product better than anyone else. Combine this with conviction, and you have a winning formula. Why? Because customers are influenced by your confidence as much as by the product itself.

Golden Formula:

Product Knowledge + Conviction = Sales

Example:

Consider a salesperson demonstrating a vacuum cleaner. If they can confidently explain its unique features, like advanced suction technology and energy efficiency, while genuinely believing in its value, the customer will sense their conviction and be more likely to buy.

How to Apply:

1. Make a list of your product's unique features and benefits.
2. Practice explaining these in simple, engaging ways.
3. Build confidence by understanding how your product solves customer problems.

Golden Statement:

"When you believe in your product, your customers will believe in you."

2. Crafting a Strong Value Proposition

A value proposition answers the customer's unspoken question: *"What's in it for me?"* It's the promise of value your product delivers and the reason a customer should choose you over competitors.

Key Elements of a Value Proposition:

1. Highlight the unique benefits of your product.
2. Address the specific pain points of your customer.
3. Use language that resonates emotionally and rationally.

Example:

If you're selling an ergonomic office chair, your value proposition might be: *"Reduce back pain and boost productivity with our scientifically designed ergonomic chairs, crafted for all-day comfort."*

Golden Statement:

"A strong value proposition is your customer's reason to say yes."

3. The Power of Lead Scoring

Not all leads are equal. Some are ready to buy, while others need nurturing. Lead scoring helps you prioritize your efforts by assigning a score to each lead based on their potential to convert.

How to Implement Lead Scoring:

1. **Hot Leads (8-10):** Ready to buy; act immediately.
2. **Warm Leads (5-7):** Interested but need nurturing through follow-ups.
3. **Cold Leads (1-4):** Unlikely to buy; keep them in your database for future campaigns.

Example:

A real estate agent might score a prospect who has attended multiple open houses and asked detailed questions as a hot lead (9). On the other hand, a casual browser on their website would score as a cold lead (3).

Golden Statement:

"Focus on hot leads to maximize results, but never ignore warm leads—they are your future customers."

4. Optimizing Average Handling Time (AHT)

Time is money in sales. Average Handling Time (AHT) measures how efficiently you interact with leads. Reducing AHT while maintaining quality can significantly boost your productivity.

Golden Formula:

AHT = (Total Time Spent on Calls + Follow-Ups) ÷ Number of Customers

Example:

A call center that averages 10 minutes per call and serves 50 customers daily will have an AHT of:

(10 × 50) ÷ 50 = 10 minutes.

By training agents to handle inquiries more effectively, they can reduce AHT to 8 minutes, increasing the number of customers served.

Golden Statement:

"Efficiency in handling time drives sales volume without compromising customer experience."

5. Understanding the Purchase Action Ratio

The journey from awareness to purchase involves four key stages:

1. **Awareness:** Making the customer aware of your product.

2. **Appeal:** Creating interest and excitement.
3. **Ask:** Encouraging the customer to take action.
4. **Act:** Closing the deal.

Golden Formula:

Purchase Action Ratio = (Number of Purchases ÷ Number of Interested Customers) × 100

Example:

A clothing store attracts 100 customers to its sale, and 25 make a purchase. The Purchase Action Ratio is:

(25 ÷ 100) × 100 = 25%.

Golden Statement:

"The higher your Purchase Action Ratio, the stronger your sales process."

6. The BANT Technique

BANT (Budget, Authority, Need, Timeline) is a framework for qualifying leads. It ensures you focus on customers who are ready and able to buy.

How to Apply BANT:

1. **Budget:** Does the customer have the financial capacity?
2. **Authority:** Are you speaking to the decision-maker?
3. **Need:** Does the customer require your product?
4. **Timeline:** When do they plan to buy?

Example:

A software company pitching to a large business might ask:

- **Budget:** "What's your budget for this solution?"

- **Authority:** "Who is responsible for final decisions on this purchase?"
- **Need:** "What challenges are you looking to solve?"
- **Timeline:** "When do you plan to implement this solution?"

Golden Statement:

"BANT saves time by focusing on customers who are ready to convert."

7. Building Community Partnerships

Sales is not just about individual customers—it's about creating communities that champion your product. Engaging with local or niche communities can boost word-of-mouth marketing and loyalty.

Example:

A sportswear brand partners with local fitness groups, offering discounts and sponsoring events. This builds goodwill and drives long-term sales.

Golden Statement:

"Communities create customers, and customers create sales."

8. The MEDDIC Framework for B2B Sales

For B2B sales, MEDDIC (Metrics, Economic Buyer, Decision Criteria, Decision Process, Identify Pain, Champion) is an invaluable tool for navigating complex deals.

Example:

A cloud services provider uses MEDDIC to tailor their pitch to a large corporation:

- **Metrics:** Show how their service saves costs by 20%.
- **Economic Buyer:** Target the CFO, who controls the budget.
- **Decision Criteria:** Highlight the company's need for scalability.
- **Champion:** Build a relationship with the IT manager.

Golden Statement:

"The MEDDIC framework ensures you never miss a step in the B2B sales process."

9. Resilience in MLM and Direct Sales

In multi-level marketing (MLM) and direct sales, success comes from persistence and relationship-building. Daily actions like follow-ups, meetings, and calls are critical.

Golden Statement:

"In direct sales, consistency beats intensity. Small daily actions build long-term success."

Reflection Questions

- Do you understand and believe in your product enough to transfer that conviction to customers?
- Are you leveraging tools like lead scoring or BANT to prioritize your efforts?
- How can you build partnerships or communities around your product?

Key Takeaways

1. Sales strategies provide structure and clarity, helping you close deals more effectively.
2. Formulas like AHT and Purchase Action Ratios allow you to measure and improve performance.

3. Techniques like BANT and MEDDIC focus your efforts on high-potential leads.

Golden Statement:

"A powerful strategy transforms selling from an art into a science."

Chapter 3
Advanced Sales Techniques

Introduction

Sales success isn't just about what you do—it's about how you think. Once you've mastered foundational strategies, the next step is to elevate your game with advanced techniques that delve into psychology, persistence, and customer-centricity. These strategies are designed to help you connect emotionally with customers, overcome resistance, and close deals like a seasoned professional. This chapter focuses on actionable techniques that can transform your sales performance.

1. The Power of Research

Every successful sales interaction starts with understanding your customer. Researching before reaching out not only saves time but also helps you craft a personalized pitch that resonates with their specific needs.

Golden Process:

1. **Gather Information**: Use tools like LinkedIn, company websites, and industry news to learn about your prospect.
2. **Identify Challenges**: Understand their pain points and goals.
3. **Tailor Your Approach**: Reference your findings in your pitch to build rapport.

Example:

Before pitching a marketing solution, a salesperson discovers that the potential client is struggling with low customer engagement. During the meeting, they suggest strategies tailored to solving this exact problem, instantly building credibility.

Golden Statement:

"Preparation transforms cold calls into warm conversations."

2. Emotional Decisions, Logical Justifications

Customers rarely make decisions based purely on logic. Instead, they buy emotionally and justify their choices rationally. Recognizing this pattern allows you to craft messages that appeal to both the heart and the mind.

How to Tap Into Emotions:

- Identify emotional triggers like security, pride, or convenience.

- Use storytelling to create a relatable narrative around your product.
- Follow up with logical evidence like statistics or testimonials.

Example:

A financial advisor uses an emotional story about a family securing their future through smart investments, followed by data showing the returns of similar clients. The emotional connection grabs attention, while the logic seals the deal.

Golden Formula:

Emotion + Logic = Commitment

Golden Statement:

"Speak to their emotions, then give them the logic to say yes."

3. Ninja Psychological Techniques

Advanced sales often involve subtle psychological methods that help influence customer decisions. These techniques, when used ethically, can make your message more persuasive and memorable.

Key Psychological Techniques:

- **Anchoring**: Set the tone by starting with a powerful statement.

Example: "This service can save you 30% on costs within six months."

- **Scarcity**: Highlight limited availability to create urgency.

Example: "Only three spots left in this exclusive program!"

- **Loss Aversion**: Emphasize what the customer might lose by not acting.

Example: "Without this software, you could be missing out on thousands in revenue."

Golden Statement:

"Psychology is the art of helping customers see the value they already need."

4. Mastering Follow-Ups

Follow-ups are the lifeblood of sales, yet they're often neglected. The key is persistence combined with value-driven communication. A good follow-up doesn't nag—it reminds the customer of the benefits you offer.

Golden Process:

1. **Schedule Follow-Ups**: Set reminders for consistent contact.
2. **Add Value Each Time**: Share insights, address concerns, or highlight new benefits.
3. **Stay Polite but Persistent**: Keep the tone professional and respectful.

Example:

A tech salesperson follows up with a prospect by sharing a case study of a similar company that benefited from their software. This reinforces the value of the product and keeps the conversation alive.

Golden Statement:

"The sale often happens after the fifth follow-up—don't stop at two."

5. The SPANCO Framework

SPANCO provides a clear roadmap for managing leads through the sales funnel. It stands for Suspect, Prospect, Approach, Negotiate, Close, and Order.

How to Use SPANCO:

- **Suspect**: Identify potential customers.

- **Prospect**: Qualify them based on interest and fit.
- **Approach**: Initiate contact with a tailored pitch.
- **Negotiate**: Handle objections and refine the offer.
- **Close**: Secure agreement and payment.
- **Order**: Deliver the product and ensure satisfaction.

Example:

A SaaS company tracks leads through SPANCO. For prospects in the "Negotiate" stage, they focus on addressing cost objections with flexible payment plans. For "Close," they ensure contracts are ready for immediate signing.

Golden Formula:

Sales Funnel Clarity = Higher Conversion Rates

Golden Statement:

"With SPANCO, every lead has a clear path to conversion."

6. Renewing Old Relationships

Many businesses focus solely on acquiring new customers, overlooking the value of past relationships. Reconnecting with former clients can often lead to quick wins.

How to Rekindle Relationships:

1. **Reach Out Personally**: Send personalized messages or emails.
2. **Offer Exclusive Deals**: Incentivize them to return.
3. **Ask for Feedback**: Show interest in their opinions and needs.

Example:

A gym sends an email to previous members offering a discounted annual membership if they rejoin within the next month. This approach brings back several old clients.

Golden Statement:

"Your past customers are your easiest wins—don't let them drift away."

Reflection Questions

1. How much time do you spend researching your customers before reaching out?
2. Are you leveraging emotional and psychological techniques effectively?
3. Do you have a structured follow-up process to nurture leads?

Key Takeaways

1. Advanced sales techniques require a deeper understanding of customer psychology and behavior.
2. Tools like SPANCO help organize and streamline your sales process.
3. Follow-ups and renewed relationships are vital for sustaining long-term success.

Golden Statement:

"The difference between good and great salespeople lies in the mastery of advanced techniques."

Chapter 4
Digital Strategies for Success

Introduction

The digital revolution has reshaped the way businesses operate, and sales is no exception. The modern customer is online—researching products, comparing options, and making purchasing decisions with just a few clicks. To succeed in this digital era, businesses must adapt by leveraging online tools and strategies that maximize visibility, engagement, and conversions.

This chapter explores actionable digital strategies that can transform your sales process, from creating a strong online presence to using powerful tools to track and optimize performance.

1. Transitioning from Offline to Online

In today's fast-paced world, businesses can no longer rely solely on traditional, offline methods. Moving operations online is essential for scaling sales, improving efficiency, and reaching a global audience.

Golden Process:

1. **Build an Online Store**: Platforms like Shopify or WooCommerce make it easy to set up a professional e-commerce website.
2. **Leverage Marketplaces**: Join popular platforms like Amazon, Flipkart, or Etsy to access a ready-made audience.
3. **Social Media Presence**: Use Facebook, Instagram, and LinkedIn to engage with customers and showcase your products.

Example:

A small boutique shifts to an online store during a festive season. With targeted ads and an engaging social media campaign, they triple their sales within two months.

Golden Statement:

"Your online presence is your new storefront—make it inviting and accessible."

2. Social Media: More Than Likes and Shares

Social media isn't just a platform for connecting with friends—it's a powerful sales tool. By strategically using social media, you can build relationships, drive engagement, and convert followers into loyal customers.

Golden Strategies for Social Media Success:

1. **Consistent Content**: Post regularly to stay on your audience's radar.

2. **Interactive Campaigns**: Use polls, contests, and live videos to engage followers.
3. **Social Proof**: Share testimonials, reviews, and user-generated content to build trust.

Example:

A fitness trainer uses Instagram to share short workout videos and tips. By offering a free guide to followers, they build an email list of potential clients and eventually launch a successful online course.

Golden Statement:

"Social media isn't about selling—it's about storytelling."

3. Creating High-Converting Landing Pages

A landing page is the first impression your potential customers get after clicking on your ad or link. Its sole purpose is to convert visitors into customers by delivering a clear and compelling message.

Golden Formula for Landing Page Success:

1. **Headline**: Catch the reader's attention immediately.

Example: "Discover the Secret to Doubling Your Productivity!"

2. **Visuals**: Use high-quality images or videos to showcase your product.
3. **Call to Action (CTA)**: Include a clear and persuasive CTA, such as "Sign Up Now" or "Buy Today."
4. **Trust Elements**: Add testimonials, certifications, or guarantees to build credibility.

Example:

An online bakery creates a landing page for its Valentine's Day special. With a catchy headline, mouth-watering photos, and a limited-time discount, the page achieves a 40% conversion rate.

Golden Statement:

"Your landing page should be a silent salesperson—clear, concise, and convincing."

4. Leveraging Free Tools for Maximum ROI

You don't need a massive budget to succeed online. Many free tools can help you track performance, create content, and optimize your digital campaigns.

Essential Free Tools for Digital Success:

1. **Google Analytics**: Track website traffic and user behavior.
2. **Canva**: Create stunning graphics for social media and ads.
3. **HubSpot CRM**: Manage customer interactions and leads.
4. **Mailchimp**: Start basic email campaigns to nurture leads.

Example:

A startup uses Canva to design professional-looking social media posts. Combined with Google Analytics to track ad performance, they optimize their campaigns without spending a dime.

Golden Statement:

"The best tools don't have to cost you—they just have to work for you."

5. Viral Marketing: The Holy Grail of Digital Sales

Viral content can catapult your brand into the spotlight, generating massive engagement and sales with minimal investment. However, going viral isn't just luck—it requires strategy.

Golden Steps to Going Viral:

1. **Relatability**: Create content that resonates with your audience's emotions.
2. **Surprise Factor**: Include an unexpected twist or humor.
3. **Call to Share**: Encourage viewers to share your content with their networks.
4. **Timeliness**: Leverage trending topics or seasonal themes.

Example:

A small café creates a video of a barista performing latte art in the shape of famous cartoon characters. The video goes viral, attracting new customers from across the city.

Golden Statement:

"Viral content isn't created by chance—it's crafted with purpose."

6. The Email Funnel Strategy

Email remains one of the most effective tools for digital sales. An email funnel guides potential customers from awareness to purchase through a series of strategic messages.

Golden Funnel Structure:

1. **Welcome Email**: Introduce your brand and provide a free resource or offer.
2. **Educational Emails**: Share tips, stories, or case studies to build trust.
3. **Exclusive Offer Email**: Present a limited-time discount or bonus.

4. **Closing Email**: Create urgency with phrases like "Last Chance" or "Offer Ends Today."

Example:

An online course creator uses an email funnel to nurture leads. After a free webinar, they send a sequence of emails that educate and entice, resulting in a 20% conversion rate.

Golden Statement:

"Every email should move the customer one step closer to saying yes."

Reflection Questions

1. Have you established a strong online presence that aligns with your brand?

2. Are you using social media to engage with your audience, not just sell to them?
3. Are your landing pages optimized for conversions with clear CTAs and trust elements?
4. Are you taking full advantage of free tools to enhance your digital strategy?

Key Takeaways

1. Moving your business online is no longer optional—it's essential.
2. Social media is a storytelling platform where trust and engagement drive sales.
3. Landing pages and email funnels are your most powerful tools for converting online leads.
4. Free tools and strategic content creation can yield impressive results with minimal investment.

Golden Statement:

"In the digital age, your sales strategy is only as strong as your online presence."

Chapter 5
Online Sales Tools

Introduction

In the digital age, success in sales depends on more than just having a great product or service. It requires leveraging the right tools to streamline your processes, track your progress, and outmaneuver the competition. Online sales tools help you manage customer interactions, monitor performance, and optimize every stage of the sales journey.

This chapter explores essential tools and strategies for enhancing your online sales efforts, ensuring that you stay ahead in an increasingly competitive landscape.

1. Tracking Competitors Online

Understanding your competitors' strategies can provide valuable insights into your market. By analyzing their online presence, pricing, and customer interactions, you can identify opportunities to differentiate your offerings.

Golden Process for Competitor Analysis:

1. **Identify Your Key Competitors**: Use tools like SEMrush or Google Search to find businesses targeting the same audience.
2. **Analyze Their Digital Presence**: Evaluate their website, social media, and online ads.
3. **Learn From Their Strengths and Weaknesses**: Identify gaps in their strategy and areas where you can outperform them.

Example:

An online bookstore discovers that a competitor is not offering book bundles. By introducing discounted bundles for popular series, they capture a new segment of customers.

Golden Statement:

"Your competitors are your best teachers—study them to surpass them."

2. Managing Your Online Reputation

Your online reputation can make or break your sales. Customers often rely on reviews and testimonials to make purchasing decisions. Managing your reputation involves monitoring feedback and addressing issues promptly.

Golden Tools for Reputation Management:

1. **Google Alerts**: Set alerts for mentions of your brand or products.

2. **Trustpilot and Yelp**: Encourage satisfied customers to leave reviews.
3. **Hootsuite**: Monitor and respond to social media mentions in real time.

Example:

A small restaurant notices a negative review about long waiting times on Yelp. They respond promptly, apologize, and offer a discount for the customer's next visit. This gesture improves their overall rating and customer trust.

Golden Statement:

"Your reputation is your silent salesperson—nurture it carefully."

3. *Using CRMs to Build Relationships*

A Customer Relationship Management (CRM) system helps you organize and track your interactions with leads and customers. It ensures no lead falls through the cracks and allows you to nurture long-term relationships.

Golden Features of a CRM:

1. **Lead Tracking**: Monitor where each lead is in the sales funnel.
2. **Automated Reminders**: Set follow-up alerts to stay on track.
3. **Data Insights**: Analyze customer behavior and preferences.

Popular CRM Tools:

- HubSpot CRM
- Salesforce
- Zoho CRM

Example:

A fitness studio uses a CRM to track prospective clients who attended free trials. Automated reminders prompt follow-ups, leading to a 30% increase in membership conversions.

Golden Statement:

"A good CRM doesn't just manage customers—it builds loyalty."

4. Email Marketing: Automating Engagement

Email marketing remains one of the most effective ways to nurture leads and drive sales. Tools like Mailchimp and ConvertKit allow you to automate campaigns, segment audiences, and track results.

Golden Steps for Email Campaign Success:

1. **Segment Your Audience**: Group leads based on interests, location, or behavior.
2. **Craft Personalized Messages**: Use the recipient's name and tailor content to their preferences.

3. **Test and Optimize**: Experiment with subject lines, content, and send times to improve engagement.

Example:

An e-learning platform segments its audience into students and professionals. By sending targeted course recommendations, they achieve a 40% open rate and increased conversions.

Golden Statement:

"Email isn't just communication—it's connection."

5. *Boosting Productivity with Automation Tools*

Automation tools save time and reduce manual effort, allowing you to focus on high-value activities. From scheduling social media posts to automating data entry, these tools enhance efficiency.

Golden Automation Tools for Sales:

1. **Zapier**: Connects apps to automate tasks like transferring leads from forms to your CRM.
2. **Calendly**: Simplifies scheduling meetings with prospects.
3. **Buffer**: Automates social media posting.

Example: A real estate agent uses Calendly to automate appointment bookings. By eliminating back-and-forth emails, they save hours each week, enabling more time for client interactions.

Golden Statement:

"Automation frees your time for what truly matters—building relationships."

6. Data Analytics for Smarter Decisions

In the digital sales ecosystem, data is power. Analytics tools provide insights into customer behavior, campaign performance, and market trends, helping you make informed decisions.

Golden Tools for Data Analytics:

1. **Google Analytics**: Tracks website traffic and user behavior.
2. **Hotjar**: Visualizes user interactions with heatmaps and session recordings.
3. **Tableau**: Creates visual dashboards to analyze complex data.

Example:

An online clothing retailer uses Google Analytics to discover that most visitors drop off on the payment page. They simplify the checkout process, reducing cart abandonment rates by 20%.

Golden Statement:

"Data isn't just numbers—it's the story of your customers."

7. Integrating All Your Tools

Using multiple tools can become overwhelming if they aren't connected. Integration ensures your systems work seamlessly, providing a unified view of your sales process.

Golden Steps for Integration:

1. **Choose Compatible Tools**: Opt for platforms that offer integrations, like Zapier or native APIs.
2. **Centralize Data**: Ensure all tools feed data into a central dashboard or CRM.
3. **Automate Workflows**: Link tools to automate repetitive tasks, such as updating lead statuses or sending follow-ups.

Example:

A travel agency integrates its CRM, email marketing tool, and social media scheduler. Leads from Instagram ads are automatically added to their CRM, triggering personalized email campaigns.

Golden Statement:

"Integrated tools create a symphony of efficiency."

Reflection Questions

1. Are you tracking your competitors to identify opportunities for improvement?
2. Is your online reputation helping or hindering your sales?
3. Are you using CRMs and automation tools effectively to streamline your process?
4. How are you using data analytics to refine your sales strategies?

Key Takeaways

1. Online sales tools help you manage leads, improve efficiency, and stay competitive.
2. CRMs are essential for nurturing relationships and tracking the customer's journey.
3. Automation saves time, while analytics provide actionable insights.
4. Integration ensures a seamless workflow, reducing errors and boosting productivity.

Golden Statement:

"The right tools transform good sales teams into great ones."

Chapter 6
Sales Closing Techniques

Introduction

The close is the most critical phase of the sales process. It's where all your efforts—building trust, demonstrating value, and addressing objections—culminate in a final decision. Closing a sale effectively requires finesse, confidence, and strategy. This chapter explores proven techniques to help you seal the deal with finesse, ensuring your customers walk away satisfied and committed.

1. Understanding the Closing Process

Closing a sale isn't just about asking for the order; it's about creating a natural progression where the customer feels confident and excited to proceed. Effective closers:

1. Build rapport throughout the interaction.
2. Address objections before they arise.
3. Create a sense of urgency or exclusivity.

Golden Statement:

"Closing isn't the end of the sale—it's the beginning of a relationship."

2. The Art of Trial Closes

A trial close is a subtle way to gauge the customer's readiness to buy without pressuring them. It allows you to test the waters and uncover any lingering concerns.

Golden Examples of Trial Closes:

- **"How does this solution align with your needs so far?"**
- **"Do you feel this product solves your challenges?"**

- **"When would you like to get started?"**

Example:

A furniture salesperson might ask, "Would you prefer the three-seater or the corner sofa for your living room?" If the customer responds positively, they are likely ready to buy.

Golden Statement:

"A trial close clears the path to the final yes."

3. Conditional Closes

A conditional close links the customer's agreement to a specific condition, making it easier for them to commit. It's particularly useful when customers are hesitant about certain aspects.

Golden Process for Conditional Closes:

1. Identify the customer's primary concern.
2. Offer a solution tied to their agreement.

3. Reinforce the benefits of proceeding.

Example:

A car dealer addressing a customer's hesitation about financing might say, "If I can secure a loan with a lower interest rate, would you be ready to proceed today?"

Golden Statement:

"Meet your customer halfway, and they'll walk the rest of the journey with you."

4. The Assumptive Close

This technique assumes the customer is ready to buy and transitions smoothly into the next steps. It's effective when the customer has shown strong interest and few objections.

Golden Steps for the Assumptive Close:

1. Act naturally confident, as if the decision has already been made.

2. Transition directly into discussing delivery, payment, or other next steps.
3. Observe the customer's response to ensure alignment.

Example:

A tech salesperson might say, "I'll set up the software on your account today so you can start exploring its features."

Golden Statement:

"Confidence in your close inspires confidence in your customer."

5. The Scarcity Close

Creating urgency can prompt customers to act quickly, especially if they are hesitant or undecided. The scarcity close emphasizes limited availability or time-sensitive offers.

Golden Formula for the Scarcity Close:

1. Highlight the urgency: "This offer is valid only until the end of the day."
2. Reinforce the exclusivity: "We have only three units left in stock."
3. Encourage action: "Let's secure this deal before it's gone."

Example:

An event planner offering a discount on their package might say, "We have only one slot left for your preferred date. Let's lock it in today."

Golden Statement:

"Urgency drives decisions—don't let hesitation hold back the close."

6. The Alternate Close

The alternate close provides the customer with two positive options, guiding them to make a decision without feeling pressured.

Golden Examples of Alternate Closes:

- "Would you prefer the annual subscription or the monthly plan?"
- "Shall we deliver the product to your office or home address?"

Example: A travel agent might ask, "Do you want to book the deluxe room with a view or the standard room closer to the amenities?"

Golden Statement:

"Giving options empowers customers to make decisions confidently."

7. Handling Objections with Empathy

Objections during the close are opportunities, not obstacles. Addressing them effectively shows your understanding of the customer's concerns and builds trust.

Golden Process for Handling Objections:

1. **Listen Actively**: Let the customer fully express their concern.
2. **Acknowledge the Concern**: Validate their feelings by saying, "That's a good point."
3. **Provide a Solution**: Offer a clear and reassuring answer to their objection.

Example:

If a customer says, "This feels expensive," a salesperson might respond, "I understand that budget is a concern. Let me show you how this investment pays for itself within three months through cost savings."

Golden Statement:

"Every objection is a chance to reaffirm your value."

8. Using AIDA to Close Effectively

AIDA stands for Attention, Interest, Desire, and Action. This classic sales framework can guide your approach to closing by ensuring you've addressed each step.

Golden Steps of AIDA:

1. **Attention**: Capture the customer's focus with a compelling introduction.
2. **Interest**: Highlight how your product meets their needs.
3. **Desire**: Build emotional engagement through stories or testimonials.
4. **Action**: End with a clear call to action, such as signing an agreement or making a payment.

Example:

A fitness coach captures attention with a bold claim ("Lose 10 pounds in 30 days!"), builds interest by explaining their program, creates desire by sharing a transformation story, and closes with a sign-up link.

Golden Statement:

"AIDA isn't just a framework—it's a roadmap to every successful close."

Reflection Questions

1. Which closing technique aligns best with your sales style and audience?
2. How do you currently handle objections during the closing process?
3. Are you consistently creating urgency and offering positive options to customers?

Key Takeaways

1. Effective closing techniques require confidence, empathy, and strategy.

2. Tools like trial closes, conditional closes, and the AIDA framework ensure you're addressing customer concerns at every step.
3. Handling objections with empathy can turn hesitation into commitment.

Golden Statement: *"The best closers don't push—they guide."*

Chapter 7
Building Customer Loyalty

Introduction

Winning a customer is just the beginning; keeping them loyal is the ultimate goal. Customer loyalty not only ensures repeat business but also transforms satisfied buyers into brand advocates. In a world where competition is fierce, loyal customers are your most valuable asset. This chapter explores strategies and techniques to build strong, lasting relationships with your customers and create a loyal customer base that fuels long-term success.

1. The Importance of Customer Retention

Acquiring new customers is significantly more expensive than retaining existing ones. Loyal customers also tend to spend more, refer others, and stick with your brand during tough times.

Golden Formula:

Customer Retention Rate = ((CE - CN) / CS) × 100

- **CE**: Customers at the end of the period.
- **CN**: New customers acquired during the period.
- **CS**: Customers at the start of the period.

Example: If you start with 100 customers, gain 20 new ones, and end with 110, your retention rate is:

((110 - 20) / 100) × 100 = 90%

Golden Statement:

"Retained customers are the foundation of sustainable growth."

2. Building Emotional Connections

Loyalty isn't just about transactions—it's about relationships. Emotional connections create a sense of trust and belonging, encouraging customers to stick with your brand.

Golden Strategies for Emotional Loyalty:

1. **Personalization**: Use names, preferences, and past purchases in your communication.
2. **Storytelling**: Share the story behind your brand to make it relatable.
3. **Customer Appreciation**: Acknowledge loyalty with thank-you messages or exclusive rewards.

Example:

A boutique hotel remembers a returning guest's preference for a specific room and welcomes them with a handwritten note. This thoughtful gesture fosters loyalty and positive word-of-mouth.

Golden Statement:

"Customers may forget what you sold them, but they'll never forget how you made them feel."

3. Creating a Loyalty Program

A well-designed loyalty program rewards repeat customers and encourages them to continue choosing your brand.

Golden Process for Designing a Loyalty Program:

1. **Define Goals**: Decide what you want to achieve—more frequent purchases, higher spend per transaction, or referrals.
2. **Choose a Reward System**: Points, discounts, freebies, or exclusive access.
3. **Promote the Program**: Make sure customers know about the benefits and how to join.

Example: A coffee shop offers a loyalty card where customers earn a free drink after every 10 purchases. This simple program keeps customers coming back.

Golden Statement:

"Loyalty isn't demanded—it's rewarded."

4. Offering Discounts and Schemes

Strategic discounts and schemes can attract new customers and retain existing ones. The key is to design offers that provide value without devaluing your product.

Golden Types of Discounts:

1. **Volume Discounts**: Offer lower prices for bulk purchases.
2. **Loyalty Discounts**: Reward returning customers with exclusive deals.
3. **Flash Sales**: Create urgency with time-limited offers.

Example:

An online retailer runs a 24-hour flash sale on select products, driving a spike in sales and attracting attention to their store.

Golden Statement:

"Discounts drive sales when they're strategic, not desperate."

5. Leveraging Feedback to Improve

Loyal customers are an invaluable source of feedback. Listening to their suggestions and addressing their concerns shows you value their input and fosters loyalty.

Golden Process for Collecting Feedback:

1. **Surveys**: Use tools like Google Forms or Typeform to gather insights.
2. **Direct Conversations**: Engage customers through emails or calls.
3. **Social Media**: Monitor comments and messages for real-time feedback.

Example:

A SaaS company regularly surveys its users about new features. By implementing the most-requested changes, they demonstrate that customer opinions matter, boosting loyalty.

Golden Statement:

"Feedback isn't criticism—it's a roadmap to improvement."

6. Creating Community Around Your Brand

Loyalty thrives in communities where customers feel connected to your brand and each other. By fostering a sense of belonging, you encourage customers to stay loyal and even advocate for your business.

Golden Strategies for Community Building:

1. **Host Events**: Organize webinars, meetups, or workshops.
2. **Create Online Groups**: Use platforms like Facebook Groups or Discord to engage your audience.

3. **Encourage User-Generated Content**: Ask customers to share their experiences with your product.

Example:

A fitness brand creates an online community where customers share workout tips, success stories, and motivation. This strengthens their connection to the brand and promotes loyalty.

Golden Statement:

"Community transforms customers into brand ambassadors."

Reflection Questions

1. Are you retaining customers effectively, or are you overly focused on acquiring new ones?

2. How are you making customers feel valued and appreciated?
3. Are you actively using feedback to improve your products or services?
4. Have you created a sense of community around your brand?

Key Takeaways

1. Customer loyalty drives repeat business and reduces the cost of acquiring new customers.
2. Emotional connections and personalized experiences foster lasting relationships.
3. Loyalty programs, discounts, and community engagement strengthen bonds with customers.
4. Listening to feedback and implementing improvements show customers that you value them.

Golden Statement: *"Loyalty isn't just a customer trait—it's a reward for consistent value and connection.*

Chapter 8
Discounts and Schemes

Introduction

Discounts and promotional schemes are powerful tools for driving sales, attracting new customers, and retaining existing ones. However, when used haphazardly, they can devalue your product and erode profits. This chapter focuses on designing strategic discounts and schemes that create excitement, build loyalty, and enhance customer value while maintaining your bottom line.

1. The Role of Discounts in Sales

Discounts serve multiple purposes:

1. **Attracting New Customers**: Special offers pique interest and encourage first-time buyers.

2. **Encouraging Repeat Purchases**: Discounts reward loyalty and keep customers coming back.
3. **Clearing Inventory**: Seasonal or clearance sales help you move unsold stock.

Golden Statement:

"A discount isn't a loss—it's an investment in future sales."

2. Types of Discounts

Different types of discounts work for different scenarios. Choosing the right type ensures you achieve your sales goals without undermining value.

Golden Types of Discounts:

1. **Flash Sales**: Time-limited offers create urgency.

Example: A clothing store announces a 50% off sale for 24 hours, driving a surge in traffic.

2. **Volume Discounts**: Encourage bulk purchases by offering lower prices for larger orders.

Example: A wholesaler provides a 10% discount on orders above $1,000.

3. **Seasonal Discounts**: Leverage holidays or seasons to create themed promotions.

Example: A fitness brand offers discounts on gym memberships during New Year's resolutions season.

4. **Bundle Offers**: Combine products at a discounted rate to increase overall spend.

Example: "Buy 2, Get 1 Free" on skincare products.

5. **Loyalty Discounts**: Reward repeat customers with exclusive deals.

Example: A café offers 20% off for loyalty cardholders.

Golden Statement:

"The right discount at the right time can spark a buying frenzy."

3. Crafting Effective Schemes

Promotional schemes extend beyond discounts to include creative incentives like contests, free trials, and cashback offers. These schemes enhance perceived value and attract attention.

Golden Promotional Schemes:

1. **Cashback Offers**: Refund a percentage of the purchase to encourage spending.

Example: An e-commerce site offers 10% cashback on payments made via specific credit cards.

2. **Contests and Giveaways**: Create excitement and engage customers.

Example: "Share your best recipe using our product for a chance to win a free cooking class!"

3. **Referral Programs**: Reward customers for bringing in new business.

Example: "Refer a friend and both get $10 off your next purchase."

4. **Trial Periods**: Let customers experience your product risk-free.

Example: A software company offers a 30-day free trial to convert hesitant leads into paying customers.

Golden Statement: *"Schemes aren't just offers—they're experiences that build trust."*

4. Avoiding the Discount Trap

While discounts can boost sales, overusing them can devalue your product and harm profitability. The key is to strike a balance between offering value and maintaining perceived quality.

Golden Rules to Avoid the Discount Trap:

1. **Set a Clear Objective**: Know why you're offering a discount—attracting new customers, clearing stock, or increasing volume.
2. **Limit the Frequency**: Too many discounts can train customers to wait for sales instead of buying at regular prices.
3. **Monitor Profit Margins**: Ensure your discounts don't eat into profits. Use formulas to calculate break-even points.

Golden Formula:

Break-Even Sales Increase (%) = (Discount % / (100% - Discount %)) × 100

Example:

For a 20% discount, the break-even sales increase is:

(20 / (100 - 20)) × 100 = 25%

This means you need a 25% increase in sales volume to maintain profitability.

Golden Statement:

"A strategic discount strengthens your brand; an excessive one weakens it."

5. Measuring the Impact of Discounts

Tracking the effectiveness of discounts ensures you're achieving your desired outcomes without sacrificing profitability.

Golden Metrics to Monitor:

1. **Conversion Rate**: Measure how many customers purchased during the discount period.
2. **Customer Lifetime Value (CLV)**: Assess whether the discount attracts loyal, repeat customers.

3. **Incremental Revenue**: Calculate the additional revenue generated from the promotion.
4. **Profit Margins**: Ensure discounts are sustainable in the long run.

Example: An electronics retailer tracks a Black Friday sale and discovers that while the discount increased sales by 40%, profit margins fell below target. They adjust future campaigns to offer slightly lower discounts and maintain profitability.

Golden Statement:

"Data-driven discounts are profitable discounts."

6. Using Discounts to Build Loyalty

Discounts aren't just for short-term gains—they can also deepen customer relationships and foster loyalty when used thoughtfully.

Golden Strategies for Loyalty-Building Discounts:

1. **Exclusive Offers for Existing Customers**: Make your loyal customers feel valued with deals unavailable to others.

Example: "Special VIP Sale: 30% Off for Members Only!"

2. **Milestone Discounts**: Celebrate anniversaries or birthdays with personalized offers.

Example: "Happy 1-Year Anniversary with Us! Enjoy 25% Off Your Next Purchase."

3. **Upsell Discounts**: Encourage customers to explore higher-value products.

Example: "Upgrade to Premium for just $10 more and enjoy additional benefits."

Golden Statement:

"Loyalty-driven discounts build connections, not just transactions."

Reflection Questions

1. Are your discounts aligned with specific business goals, such as customer acquisition or inventory clearance?
2. Are you tracking the financial impact of your promotions to ensure profitability?
3. How can you use discounts to build long-term customer relationships instead of just short-term sales?

Key Takeaways

1. Discounts and schemes are powerful tools for driving sales, but they must be used strategically.
2. Effective promotions balance customer value with business profitability.
3. Measuring the impact of discounts helps you refine your strategies for long-term success.
4. Loyalty-driven discounts build trust and deepen customer relationships.

Golden Statement:

"Smart discounts don't just sell products—they build brands."

Chapter 9
Customer-Centric Sales

Introduction

The modern customer expects more than a transaction—they expect a relationship. Customer-centric sales prioritize the needs, preferences, and challenges of the buyer, ensuring that every interaction delivers value. This approach doesn't just close deals; it builds trust and fosters loyalty. In this chapter, we'll explore how to tailor your sales strategies to put the customer at the center of every decision, creating win-win outcomes that drive long-term success.

1. Understanding Customer-Centric Selling

Customer-centric selling is about shifting the focus from the product to the customer.

Instead of asking, "How can I sell this?" ask, "How can I solve this customer's problem?"

Golden Principles of Customer-Centric Selling:

1. **Empathy**: Understand the customer's pain points and goals.
2. **Customization**: Tailor your approach to meet individual needs.
3. **Value Creation**: Focus on how your product or service enhances their life or business.

Golden Statement:

"Customer-centric sales don't push products—they offer solutions."

2. Consultative Selling: Being a Trusted Advisor

Consultative selling involves guiding the customer through the decision-making process by acting as an advisor rather than a salesperson. This approach positions you as a partner invested in their success.

Golden Process for Consultative Selling:

1. **Ask Insightful Questions**: Understand the customer's needs and challenges.

Example: "What's your biggest obstacle to achieving [specific goal] right now?"

2. **Listen Actively**: Pay attention to their responses and clarify when necessary.
3. **Recommend Thoughtfully**: Offer tailored solutions based on their answers.

Example:

A financial advisor uses consultative selling to understand a client's retirement goals. Instead of pitching generic investment plans, they recommend a custom portfolio aligned with the client's risk tolerance and timeline.

Golden Statement:

"Be the advisor they trust, not the salesperson they avoid."

3. Creating Value Beyond Products

Customers value brands that go beyond selling to provide additional benefits. By offering educational content, actionable insights, or exceptional support, you position yourself as a valuable resource.

Golden Strategies for Creating Value:

1. **Educate**: Share tips, tutorials, or industry insights.

Example: A skincare brand creates a blog with articles on managing different skin types.

2. **Solve Problems**: Provide tools or resources that address common challenges.

Example: A software company offers free templates to simplify project management.

3. **Be Available**: Ensure quick and reliable customer support.

Golden Statement:

"Value is the currency of trust."

4. Personalizing the Sales Experience

Personalization makes customers feel valued and understood. By tailoring your approach to their preferences, you enhance the likelihood of a successful sale.

Golden Process for Personalization:

1. **Leverage Data**: Use CRM tools to track customer history and preferences.
2. **Customize Communication**: Address customers by name and reference their specific needs.
3. **Adapt Your Offer**: Highlight features or benefits that matter most to them.

Example:

An online retailer sends personalized emails recommending products based on a customer's past purchases, resulting in higher engagement and repeat sales.

Golden Statement:

"Personalization isn't a feature—it's a necessity."

5. Using the Golden Circle for Customer-Centricity

Simon Sinek's **Golden Circle** framework—*Why, How, What*—is a powerful tool for customer-centric sales.

Golden Circle Explained:

1. **Why**: Start with the purpose behind your product or service.

Example: "We believe in making education accessible to everyone."

2. **How**: Explain how your product achieves this purpose.

Example: "Our online platform offers affordable courses that fit any schedule."

3. **What**: Finally, present the product itself.

Example: "Here's our course catalog designed for working professionals."

Golden Statement:

"Start with the why, and the what will sell itself."

6. Handling Rejections Gracefully

Rejections are inevitable, but how you respond to them can make all the difference. A graceful response shows professionalism and keeps the door open for future opportunities.

Golden Process for Handling Rejections:

1. **Stay Positive**: Thank the customer for their time and feedback.

2. **Seek Feedback**: Ask what factors influenced their decision.
3. **Follow Up Later**: Reconnect with them in the future with updated offerings.

Example:

A salesperson follows up with a prospect who initially declined a service, sharing a new feature tailored to their needs. The prospect reconsiders and makes a purchase.

Golden Statement:

"A no today could be a yes tomorrow—handle it with care."

7. Measuring the Success of Customer-Centric Strategies

To ensure your approach is working, track metrics that reflect customer satisfaction and loyalty.

Golden Metrics to Monitor:

1. **Customer Satisfaction Score (CSAT)**: Measure how happy customers are with your service.
2. **Net Promoter Score (NPS)**: Gauge how likely customers are to recommend your brand.
3. **Customer Lifetime Value (CLV)**: Assess the total revenue a customer brings over their relationship with your brand.

Example:

A SaaS company improves its NPS by implementing a feedback loop, addressing common concerns, and sharing updates with customers.

Golden Statement:

"The success of customer-centricity is measured in loyalty, not just sales."

Reflection Questions

1. Are you focusing on solving customer problems rather than just selling products?
2. How personalized are your sales interactions?
3. Are you tracking customer satisfaction and loyalty metrics to refine your approach?

Key Takeaways

1. Customer-centric sales prioritize relationships over transactions, creating long-term value for both parties.
2. Consultative selling positions you as a trusted advisor, building trust and credibility.

3. Personalization and added value enhance the customer experience and foster loyalty.
4. Measuring satisfaction and handling rejections gracefully ensure continuous improvement.

Golden Statement:

"The more you focus on your customer's success, the more successful you'll become."

Chapter 10
Scaling Your Sales Operations

Introduction

Scaling your sales operations is a critical step toward sustainable growth. While mastering sales on a small scale is essential, expanding your operations requires structure, consistency, and efficiency. Scaling isn't just about increasing the number of sales—it's about building systems that can handle growth without compromising quality or customer experience. This chapter focuses on strategies to optimize and scale your sales processes, ensuring your business can grow seamlessly.

1. Building a Scalable Sales Framework

A scalable sales framework ensures that as your business grows, your sales processes can handle increased demand without breaking down. This involves standardizing workflows, automating repetitive tasks, and ensuring your team has the resources they need.

Golden Components of a Scalable Framework:

1. **Standard Operating Procedures (SOPs):** Document clear, repeatable steps for every aspect of the sales process.
2. **Automation Tools:** Use CRM systems, email automation, and lead scoring tools to reduce manual effort.
3. **Training Programs:** Provide consistent onboarding and upskilling for new and existing team members.

Example:

A SaaS company creates an SOP for handling inbound leads, automates follow-up emails through HubSpot, and trains new hires using video modules. This allows them to onboard new sales reps quickly and handle more leads efficiently.

Golden Statement:

"A scalable framework transforms chaos into consistency."

2. Leveraging Technology to Drive Growth

Technology is the backbone of modern sales operations. It streamlines processes, enhances communication, and provides data-driven insights that inform strategic decisions.

Golden Tools for Scaling Sales Operations:

1. **Customer Relationship Management (CRM):** Centralize lead and customer data with tools like Salesforce or Zoho CRM.
2. **Analytics Platforms:** Track performance metrics and identify growth opportunities using Google Analytics or Tableau.

3. **Communication Tools:** Use platforms like Slack or Microsoft Teams for seamless collaboration.

Example:

A real estate agency integrates Slack for team communication and Tableau for tracking agent performance. This reduces response times and improves customer satisfaction.

Golden Statement:

"The right technology doesn't just scale your operations—it amplifies your potential."

3. Expanding Your Sales Team

As your business grows, so should your sales team. Scaling your team requires more than just hiring—it involves ensuring every member aligns with your company culture and goals.

Golden Process for Expanding Your Team:

1. **Hire Strategically:** Look for candidates with experience, adaptability, and a customer-first mindset.
2. **Set Clear KPIs:** Define measurable goals for individual and team performance.
3. **Foster Collaboration:** Encourage teamwork to share insights and improve outcomes.

Example:

A fashion retailer expands its team by hiring e-commerce specialists to handle the growing volume of online orders. Clear KPIs and collaborative training sessions ensure alignment and efficiency.

Golden Statement:

"A great team doesn't just grow your sales—it grows your brand."

4. Building a Sales Culture

A strong sales culture is the foundation of a scalable sales operation. It fosters motivation, accountability, and a shared vision among your team.

Golden Pillars of a Sales Culture:

1. **Transparency:** Share goals, progress, and challenges openly.
2. **Recognition:** Celebrate individual and team achievements.
3. **Continuous Learning:** Encourage skill development through workshops and coaching.

Example:

A healthcare company organizes monthly recognition events to celebrate top performers and hosts quarterly training sessions to keep the team updated on industry trends.

Golden Statement:

"A thriving sales culture drives excellence at every level."

5. Optimizing the Sales Funnel

Scaling requires a finely tuned sales funnel that maximizes efficiency and minimizes drop-offs at every stage. Regularly analyzing and refining the funnel ensures optimal performance.

Golden Steps for Funnel Optimization:

1. **Identify Bottlenecks:** Use analytics to find stages where leads drop off.
2. **Streamline Processes:** Simplify steps to reduce friction, such as automating follow-ups.
3. **Enhance Conversion Rates:** Test new approaches like revised CTAs or updated messaging.

Example:

An online course platform notices a high drop-off rate at the checkout page. By adding a one-click payment option, they increase conversions by 25%.

Golden Statement:

"Your funnel isn't a fixed pipeline—it's a dynamic system for growth."

6. Expanding into New Markets

Scaling often involves exploring untapped markets, whether geographically or demographically. Expanding strategically ensures you maximize opportunities while minimizing risks.

Golden Steps for Market Expansion:

1. **Research the Market:** Understand customer needs, competition, and cultural nuances.

2. **Test the Waters:** Launch pilot campaigns before a full-scale entry.
3. **Adapt Your Approach:** Tailor your messaging and product offerings to fit the new market.

Example:

A beverage company expands into a new region by launching a limited edition flavor tailored to local tastes, supported by a targeted social media campaign.

Golden Statement:

"Expansion isn't about selling everywhere—it's about succeeding where you sell."

7. Measuring and Refining Success

Scaling is an ongoing process that requires regular evaluation and adjustment. By tracking key metrics, you can identify what's working, refine your strategies, and ensure sustainable growth.

Golden Metrics to Track:

1. **Customer Acquisition Cost (CAC):** The cost of acquiring a new customer.
2. **Revenue Growth Rate:** The percentage increase in revenue over time.
3. **Sales Cycle Length:** The average time it takes to close a deal.
4. **Customer Retention Rate:** The percentage of customers who continue buying from you.

Example:

A subscription box company tracks its CAC and discovers that referrals have the lowest cost. They double down on their referral program, reducing overall acquisition costs.

Golden Statement:

"Scaling isn't about doing more—it's about doing better."

Reflection Questions

1. Are your sales processes standardized and scalable?
2. Are you leveraging technology effectively to streamline operations?
3. How strong is your sales culture in fostering collaboration and excellence?
4. Are you tracking the right metrics to measure and refine your growth strategies?

Key Takeaways

1. A scalable sales framework ensures consistent performance as your business grows.
2. Technology, team expansion, and a strong sales culture are critical for scaling effectively.

3. Optimizing your sales funnel and entering new markets strategically drive sustainable growth.
4. Measuring and refining success ensures your scaling efforts deliver maximum impact.

Golden Statement:

"Scaling isn't just growth—it's growth with purpose."

Chapter 11
Conclusion and Future Directions

Introduction

Sales is more than a function—it's the heartbeat of every business. Throughout this book, we've explored strategies, techniques, and tools that can transform how you approach selling. From building a strong foundation to mastering advanced techniques and scaling your operations, the journey of sales mastery is both rewarding and challenging.

In this concluding chapter, we'll summarize the core lessons from the book and offer actionable steps to help you implement what you've learned. Whether you're just starting out or looking to refine your sales process, these insights will serve as a compass for your continued success.

1. The Core Lessons of Selling

1. Conviction and Knowledge Are Key

2. Sales begins with belief—belief in your product, your customer, and yourself. Without conviction and deep product knowledge, it's impossible to inspire trust and drive action.

3. The Customer Comes First

Customer-centric sales aren't just a strategy—they're a mindset. Focus on solving problems, building relationships, and delivering value at every touchpoint.

4. Adaptability Drives Success

The sales landscape is constantly evolving. Whether it's leveraging digital tools, embracing new techniques, or expanding into untapped markets, adaptability is your greatest asset.

Golden Statement:

"Sales mastery is a journey, not a destination."

2. Actionable Next Steps

Step 1: Review and Reflect

Take time to assess your current sales strategies. Identify what's working, what's not, and where there's room for improvement.

Reflection Questions:

- Are your processes customer-centric?
- Are you leveraging technology and tools effectively?
- Are you continuously measuring and refining your approach?

Step 2: Prioritize Implementation

Start by implementing one or two key strategies from this book that align with your goals. Focus on building momentum rather than overhauling everything at once.

Example:

If lead nurturing is a weakness, focus on creating a structured follow-up process first.

Step 3: Embrace Continuous Learning

Sales is a dynamic field that requires ongoing learning and adaptation. Commit to regular training, reading, and experimentation to stay ahead of the curve.

Example:

Set aside time each month to explore new tools, attend workshops, or read industry blogs.

Golden Statement:

"Small, consistent actions lead to monumental results."

3. The Road Ahead

As you apply these lessons, remember that sales is as much about people as it is about products. Building trust, understanding needs, and delivering value will always be at the heart of successful selling. The strategies and techniques you've learned here are tools—but your passion and dedication are what will truly drive your success.

Golden Vision for the Future:

- **For Individuals:** Aim to become not just a salesperson, but a trusted advisor who creates lasting relationships.
- **For Businesses:** Strive to build a sales culture that empowers your team, delights your customers, and drives sustainable growth.

4. Final Reflection Questions

1. What is your greatest takeaway from this book?
2. How will you implement the strategies and tools you've learned into your daily sales process?
3. What steps will you take to ensure continuous growth and improvement in your sales journey?

Key Takeaways

1. Sales success comes from a combination of skills, mindset, and adaptability.
2. Customer-centricity is the cornerstone of long-term success.
3. Scaling your operations requires structure, collaboration, and strategic planning.
4. Continuous learning and refinement ensure you stay ahead in an ever-changing marketplace.

Golden Statement: *"The art of selling is the art of building connections—with people, with value, and with success."*

Closing Words

Sales isn't just about numbers—it's about transformation. It transforms how customers solve their problems, how businesses grow, and how salespeople evolve. As you embark on or continue your sales journey, let this book be your guide, your reminder, and your source of inspiration.

Here's to your success in mastering the art of selling and transforming your business for the better.

A Message from the Author

Dear Reader,

Thank you for taking the time to embark on this journey through **"The Art of Selling: Strategies to Transform Your Business."** Writing this book has been a labor of passion and dedication, fueled by the belief that anyone can master the art of selling with the right mindset and tools.

Sales is not just about products, numbers, or goals—it's about people, connections, and transformation. As you've explored the strategies, techniques, and tools laid out in this book, I hope you've found inspiration and actionable insights that resonate with your unique journey.

I want to remind you that every great salesperson, entrepreneur, or leader started with a single step—the decision to grow. By reading this book, you've taken that step, and

I am confident that you have what it takes to achieve incredible success.

If you have questions, stories to share, or simply want to connect, I would love to hear from you. Please feel free to reach out to me at [Your Contact Information or Website]. Your feedback and experiences are invaluable and inspire me to keep creating content that adds value to lives.

Finally, I wish you immense success, joy, and fulfillment in your sales journey and beyond. May you not only transform your business but also inspire those around you to strive for greatness.

Thank you for allowing me to be a part of your story. Here's to your success!

Warm regards,

Prince Kachhadiya

Author of **"The Art of Selling: Strategies to Transform Your Business"**

THANK YOU

The Art of Selling: Strategies to Transform Your Business

By PRINCE KACHHADIYA

www.ingramcontent.com/pod-product-compliance
Lightning Source LLC
Chambersburg PA
CBHW031427210526
45464CB00005B/2092